THE LAW OF LAW SCHOOL

T0366629

The Law

of

Law School

THE ESSENTIAL GUIDE
for
First-Year Law Students

ANDREW GUTHRIE FERGUSON
and
JONATHAN YUSEF NEWTON

NEW YORK UNIVERSITY PRESS
New York

NEW YORK UNIVERSITY PRESS
New York
www.nyupress.org

References to Internet websites (URLs) were accurate at the time of writing.
Neither the author nor New York University Press is responsible for URLs
that may have expired or changed since the manuscript was prepared.

Library of Congress Cataloging-in-Publication Data
Names: Ferguson, Andrew G., author. | Newton, Jonathan, author.
Title: The law of law school : the essential guide for first-year law students /
Andrew Guthrie Ferguson, Jonathan Newton.
Description: New York : New York University Press, 2020. |
Includes bibliographical references and index. | Summary: "The Law of Law
School" serves as a guide for first-year law students"— Provided by publisher.
Identifiers: LCCN 2019033352 | ISBN 9781479801688 (cloth) |
ISBN 9781479801626 (paperback) | ISBN 9781479801619 (ebook) |
ISBN 9781479801602 (ebook)
Subjects: LCSH: Law schools—United States—Handbooks, manuals, etc. |
Law—Study and teaching—United States.
Classification: LCC KF272 .F43 2020 | DDC 340.071/173—dc23
LC record available at https://lccn.loc.gov/2019033352

New York University Press books are printed on acid-free paper, and their
binding materials are chosen for strength and durability. We strive
to use environmentally responsible suppliers and materials
to the greatest extent possible in publishing our books.

Manufactured in the United States of America

10 9 8 7 6 5 4 3 2 1

Also available as an ebook

CONTENTS

Introduction

Law comes in many forms. Sometimes it is written on old-fashioned parchment with fancy and important-sounding words. Sometimes it is bound in code with formal written rules. And sometimes it exists in between: in between cases, rulings, and theories. Such "in-between law" is not clear; it evolves, changes, and is hard to see. In law school, you will come to understand this as the common law—a process of judge-made decisions and traditions developed over history. It is a thing (although there is no way to find it in the library). You will learn about it and come to understand it, all without ever seeing it. The same is true with success in law school.

Law school itself has its own common law, and success in law school requires you to understand it. This book tries to reveal that common wisdom by distilling this common law into one hundred rules. They don't guarantee success, but they guarantee you will be well ahead of other students still trying to understand that there is a "law of law school."

Students and professors all agree on one thing: to succeed in your first year of law school you need to immerse yourself in the experience. There are rules, tips, and theories that are all different for different schools, but there are many principles that will apply generally. And just as the common law developed in different places over different times yet still can be taught as one unified whole, so certain lessons from law schools also arising from different places and different times can be distilled into rules to help you master law school. This book provides the guide.

Letter to a 1L on the First Day of Law School

Dear Law Student:

Here's the truth. You belong here. You may not always feel that you belong, but that is our fault, not yours. You see, law school is not set up like other educational experiences. It is not set up simply to teach a subject (contracts, torts, criminal law) as much as to teach a skill set—a set of competencies that will allow you to do the work of lawyering. You are not going to be given the law to memorize. You are going to be taught the skills to find the law, apply the law, make a strong argument, and then turn around and identify all of the weaknesses of that argument.

And, to be fair, there is a good reason for this method—when you graduate from law school there will be no textbooks filled with answers. If there were easy answers available in some book, people wouldn't need lawyers. No, your skill set will be to answer the question that is not yet asked and maybe not yet imagined.

But the fact that there might be a good reason to teach law this way doesn't make it any easier. It is still a puzzle game in which we—the law professors—don't always give you the clues (or even make it clear that you are solving a puzzle). The challenges are real and sometimes disempowering. You should understand where this feeling comes from as you begin the process of connecting with the law. Uncertainty in the first few weeks of law school comes from the way 1L classes have historically been taught in the United States. There are four main challenges.

First, in most first-year law school classes, you are assigned to read a series of judicial opinions organized by subject area. In criminal law, you might get cases about subjects like "punishment," "theft," or "homicide," and the cases explain legal issues arising from those subjects. But the judicial opinions were not written for you as law students. They were not written as teaching tools to explain the law. Instead, they were written to resolve a particular legal problem. The judge is writing to professional lawyers who have spent hours (if not years) arguing about a legal subject in which they have expertise and experience.

So when you—the student—sit down to read a case resolving the particular litigant's dispute, you might justifiably feel a bit lost. After all, you don't know the complete factual background of the case. You don't know the history of the law. You don't know the social and political context of the judge's decision. And no one is going to teach you. While the judge typically provides some of that information (the basic facts, law, and reasoning), the entire process is a conversation among legal experts with a tremendous amount of assumed knowledge needed to understand the case.

In the first weeks of law school, that is an odd place to be. You are thrown into a conversation in which the people aren't talking to you. You are eavesdropping, trying to join the experts in a discussion about a subject you know very little about.

To overcome this confusion, you must accept that you are joining a long-standing, ongoing conversation midstream. While you may understand some of what is being said, much of your confusion comes from the fact that the law is not written for you in your role as student but for you as a future lawyer. You are right to feel lost, but it won't stay that way.

At some point later in life, you will return to a case that you first read as a 1L, and you will discover a completely different meaning. You will see the crosscurrents of legal theory and political debate. You will understand the personalities of the judges and their backgrounds. You will know how the case fits within a larger tapestry of judge-made law and history. But none of these insights will be evident the first time you read the case or try to figure out its importance.

Worse, this challenge will be exacerbated by your professors, who often "aren't talking to you." Sure, in class the professor might be directing a pointed question your way, making your heart race, your hands sweat, and your face flush (we've all been there). But the classroom conversation is not really between the professor and the student but instead between the professor and the class. Your answers are merely a vehicle to elucidate the relevant legal rules or principles at stake. Your answers (as brilliant as you imagine them to be) have little direct bearing on the purpose of the class. The questions are the point. The questions are the answers. The questions show you how to think about the next unanswered issue: What if . . . ? What about . . . ? What is the logical stopping point for the argument? How do the rules fit a different factual setting? Your professors are talking past you, joining the ongoing conversation in the cases, connecting you to the discussion of the next case and the next. This can be confusing if you don't understand what is happening.

Second, law has its own language and is meant to be exclusionary. When you first start reading legal opinions (especially older cases from prior centuries), you will be struck by the amount of unnecessary jargon, Latin terms, and legal phrases that confuse and clutter opinions. Why, you might ask, would anyone use more complicated and sophisticated-sounding language when a simple alternative would suffice? The answer is not necessarily complimentary to the legal profession but may be understandable. The answer is "because we can" and because lawyers have been trained in a way that such language gives them the power to exclude others from the club. Professionals protect professionalism by exclusionary mechanisms so that others (not in the club) need to hire those very same professionals.

Don't judge too quickly. You will find that when you sit down to write your first law school paper, it will be filled with all the legal terms you have just mastered. You will, in fact, feel proud to write "henceforth, the substantive normative claims that reveal the gravamen of my underlying argument" when you could simply say, "because I think so." The same is true for judges and law clerks and lawyers trying to claim professionalism and expertise through language. Sure, some of the language offers a measure of precision, and some legal phrases evolved from British traditions, but much of it is just the consequence of professionals trying to express professional superiority in an effort to maintain power and control.

So understand that the first few weeks of law school are hard because you are learning a new language that is meant to exclude "the old you." Many students begin to doubt themselves because the words look like English but just don't make sense. Again, recognize that the judges are not talking like you do because they are talking like lawyers do—a skill that you have not yet learned.

In time, "the new you" will master the language of law. In time, the discomfort you feel when reading archaic language will become a point of pride. You will feel empowered because you will be able to decode the off-putting confusion of old-fashioned legalese. You will spout off definitions for words such as "curtilage" and "consideration" and know among other things what "inter alia" means (it means "among other things"). But until you gain that level of fluency, you will feel like the outsider—someone who has not yet learned the secrets of the legal profession.

Third, if you enter law school as anything other than a white male with significant socioeconomic power, you might feel something missing about the world discussed in many cases. For centuries, the law was exclusively written and interpreted by white men with significant socioeconomic power. This influence means that our core foundational legal principles were created by white men of power. This framing influenced what many judges believed to be "reasonable" behavior and what is considered an "objective" perspective.

Reading cases that reflect a narrow worldview can create discomfort for law students as they recognize that the law has often failed to acknowledge their reality and their own diversity of experiences. Students might feel erased—that their existence is not completely represented in the assumptions underlying the decisions that constitute "the law." And they would be right.

Throughout history, the law articulated in legal opinions has often served the interests of a select few at the expense of the disempowered majority. Property law legitimized the commodification of human beings. Contract law legitimized the structural imbalance of economic power.

Criminal law legitimized the subjugation of minority races and women. Many of the gravest racial, gender, and sexual-orientation injustices in our history were based on legal justifications that empowered certain groups over others.

Any law student honestly reflecting on the evolution of US law will see it as embedded with structural inequality; ignorant of racial, gender, and other societal differences; and silent about the experiences of the vast majority of the population. This truth does not delegitimize the law but instead legitimizes the feelings and lived experience of students who can see (and viscerally feel) the different and unacknowledged realities in their assigned cases.

Finally, part of the reason 1L year feels so overwhelming is that you are learning not just the law but the legal profession. The value of law school comes from learning about the culture, history, and practice of law that cannot be found in the books. Through the cases and conversations, you are learning about a culture and a profession with its own norms, traditions, and expectations.

Such an education is probably a full-time pursuit, which is sort of unfortunate because your professors are still going to demand equal time from your books. And as every practicing lawyer knows, one full-time job plus another full-time job equals just being a lawyer.

If you feel overwhelmed during your 1L year, know that it is because you have been assigned too much reading, in too many classes, on too difficult a level. This is an objective fact. Further, none of your professors will coordinate the workload, and it will only get worse as the semester goes on. Finally, the rest of life will also not stop adding all sorts of unfortunate hurdles to an already impossible task. This is what all 1Ls feel no matter where they go to school, where they came from, or where they are going. It is also survivable if you know what to expect.

A good part of success in law school (or at least sanity) turns on expectations and planning. Understanding the scope and scale of the expectations beyond just classroom assignments will enable you to plan accordingly. Law school is a holistic professional experience of which academic learning is just one part. In fact, the other parts will seem both more immediate and more interesting. I promise that while you will probably spend more time in the library with your books, the things you will remember about law school will have to do with professional experiences, events, and friendships. Law school is about all of those things, and it all takes time.

The good news is that people have been going to law school for a long time, and many of the important lessons have been identified and distilled through trial and error. People suffered so that you don't have to. This book was written to ease the suffering a bit and identify the core principles that can connect you to the otherwise disconnecting and disempowering process of 1L year.

If there is one lesson you will take away from law school, it is how to "issue spot"—that's what lawyers do. They foresee the risks ahead, understand the legal rules that cover the issues, and offer advice about those issues. This book is an issue-spotting guide to the risks of law school. It distills the possible trouble spots, posits general rules to address those issues, and then explains its reasoning. This is the same skill your professors are going to ask you to display in class or on the final exam.

You have already seen it in action. We have issue spotted the first four reasons why students feel challenged in the first few weeks of law school. You are not crazy to feel disconnected during the law school educational process. But once you see these issues as issues, you can discover ways around them.

The rules in this book seek to connect you to a path of success. By understanding the law of law school, you will be able to master the law and enjoy the law school experience. It won't be easy, but it will be done. And you will do it, because you belong here.

Sincerely,
Professor Ferguson

1L Mind-Set

There Is a "Law of Law School"

To succeed you must learn the law of law school. Rules, methods, and principles exist that guide successful students. These laws will be found (accidentally or intentionally) by every successful student.

Most people go to law school thinking that "the law" will be provided in thick, overpriced, hardbound books. But those casebooks are the tip of the proverbial iceberg. Law is vast and complicated with many thousand submerged ideas behind each selected case excerpt. Just as you must see beyond the neatly shrink-wrapped books to find the real law, so you must search for the real law of law school. There exist layers of skills, insights, and rules to find and follow.

These laws will help you navigate classes, exams, stress, and the entire immersive experience of law school. You must see the law school learning experience as a process of discovering these laws—a process that takes work, exertion, courage, and a good guide.

Discover Your School's Legal Culture

Law—be it written in statutes, regulations, cases, or constitutional text—has no force without a culture to support it. Laws are merely words without institutions to enforce them and individuals to apply them. Many lawless nations have laws on the books, but a law-bound community has a culture to support those written principles. The same is true for law school. Law school requires a culture to support its students.

As a student, you must discover how the particular culture and institutions of your school shape the law of law school. You are now part of that culture and will help to shape it. But first you must study your particular culture. Who are the deans, the administration, the staff? Where are the student support structures? Who is the law student leader? What is the governing structure? Figure out the institutional framework for how the school operates, from the registrar to the editors of the law review. Each has a role in how the school operates, and you should make a conscious decision to understand how they all fit together. The first clue to understanding a legal code is to step back and study its structure and organization. The same is true for understanding law school.

RULE 3

Law Is Personal

Law is human and real. The study of law is going to impact you personally. Laws may be written in the abstract, but they have real human impacts. Laws allow state killing. Laws allow children to be removed from their parents. Laws cover birth, marriage, death, jobs, property, belief, and liberty. You must never forget that the law has real effects on others.

Even as you figure out how to distance yourself from arguments, coldly apply logic to facts, and be the dispassionate professional you believe lawyers must be, remember that somebody probably cried because of the case, and they were right to cry. Somebody lost something precious— liberty, dignity, property, rights, family—and the law did it.

The law of law school is also personal. It will affect you and your peers. It will change how you interact with each other and with your nonlawyer friends. It will cause stress, sleeplessness, and emotional difficulty. It may try to kill you. On occasion, these negative emotions can be debilitating, and you should seek professional help if they become overwhelming.

At the same time, the law of law school will change how you think, how you communicate, and how you see the world. You will become smarter, sharper, and more valuable in whatever you end up doing. Done correctly, succeeding in law school can be a positive and personally meaningful experience. Done successfully, law school can be quite fun.

Flip Your Thinking

Learning is flipped in law school. Unlike undergraduate or high school classes, you do not come to class to learn the material. You come to class to apply the lessons you have learned yourself through your reading and studying. The American Bar Association (ABA) standards suggest that for every hour in class, you should study two hours at home.

Law students are not passive consumers but active participants in learning. You are necessarily teaching yourself the law, because that is what you do as a lawyer in a world of ever-evolving legal precedent. Lawyers answer unanswered questions for a living. This process takes work, and it also takes a commitment to struggle through the learning process. You are being asked to do something inherently difficult: teach yourself a complicated subject. 1L courses provide examples of foundational legal concepts, but the goal is not simply to learn the nuts and bolts of contracts or torts or criminal law but to learn how to master any legal subject. The skill to teach yourself is the skill you will need as a lawyer. This is the actual skill you are paying to learn in law school.

RULE 5

Think like a Lawyer

Throughout law school, people will tell you to "start thinking like a lawyer." This is frustrating and unhelpful. It is usually stated as a criticism, without any clarity of what it means. The good news is that there is no one way to think like a lawyer. The bad news is that you still have to understand the concept.

In general, thinking like a lawyer means thinking about a problem in a particular way—one that involves identifying a precise issue, identifying the rule that goes with the issue, analyzing it, evaluating the problem objectively from both sides, and then offering a conclusion. In short:

- Identify the issue.
- Identify the rule.
- Identify the relevant facts.
- Apply the facts to the rule.
- Conclude.
- Argue the other side of the argument.
- Choose the best of those two options.
- Find the next issue.
- Repeat.

You will find that this way of thinking is helpful for resolving questions on an exam and arguing about the best new restaurant or hot-button political issue. It will also make you insufferable around your nonlawyer friends and family.

Planning
to Plan

Plan for "Day One" of Law School

"Day One" represents the beginning of law school. But here is the trick. If you wait to plan on the actual first day, you are already behind. One of the first lessons of law school is that words don't always mean what they say. "Reading period" sounds like a time you read rather than the few days you frantically catch up and cram several major subjects into your brain. "Thanksgiving" used to be a holiday you spend with family. Now it will be a time to finish outlining before the fun of reading period.

Day One is the day you are mentally prepared to embark on the path to law school success. It could be weeks before the first day of school. Day One involves the preparation moment when you affirmatively attack your work. Law school (and law) is not a passive enterprise. Things don't come to you. You plan, develop, and then implement the plan.

By Day One, you must have your books, study aids, computer, a plan for the semester, and your schedule to attack the first class and the first reading.

There Is No "Day Two"

There is no "Day Two" in law school, only repetitive Day Ones. Every day you should mentally recheck, plan, and get ready to attack your studies. If you are not prepared, you are behind.

The reason to be prepared on Day One is that you cannot be sure there will be other moments to plan. One of the most frustrating things about 1L year is that you cannot foresee the challenges ahead. You will constantly feel like you are jumping through ever-multiplying hoops. But you won't see the hoops in the beginning. They will come in the form of assignments, opportunities, and life challenges. Many will take longer than planned. Some will not be choices. All will make you a better lawyer. The key to Day One planning is recognizing that there will always be another hoop ahead and that you need to accomplish the things you can now, because there might not be a time later on.

Visualize the Full Semester

Law school semesters have a rhythm. 1L year begins chaotically, with a flood of orientation information and then a crush of reading and preparing for class. After a few weeks, things appear to ease up a bit, allowing for a false hope of balance. Then the testing begins, first with midterms, then writing assignments, outlines, practice tests, and a host of other requirements. The semester crescendos with final exams, and if you do it correctly, there is never a letup until the final moments of the final exam.

Knowing this pattern (ahead of time) allows you to plan for the full semester and avoid the pitfalls. You cannot put off your work until the end, because the work does not stop. In fact, the readings only increase as professors get behind on their class assignments and end-of-the-semester writing projects or extracurricular obligations begin taking all your time. You must see ahead of the curve to account for the unforeseen but always inevitable increase in work.

Be prepared for the crescendo that is coming.

Don't Forsake Free Help

During your first weeks of law school, you will be inundated by a variety of free study aids and digital platforms to use during your law school career. Many students will wait until the middle of the semester to sign up for these free online resources. Do not wait!

Included in many of these resources are not only secondary source matter but access to study aids, black-letter law outlines, and more. (Black-letter law is just the well-established understanding of core legal rules.) Some providers even have free video lectures of core 1L subjects as part of their offering. In addition, a few of the vendors provide free study aids that cost money to obtain otherwise. Study aids are simply books or digital materials that try to break down the information in an easily digestible way. The value of these resources to a law student is immeasurable.

In addition, law schools have professional academic success programs designed to help you. Professors who have studied, mastered, and thought about how to help students learn the law are in the building. Go to them. Seek them out. Learn. You have experts who have devoted their careers to this particular skill set just waiting for you to introduce yourself. Academic success professors may be the most important professors you meet. Find them and seek their guidance. Remember that you are not the first law student embarking on this path. There exists an entire supportive infrastructure to help you find your way.

Plan for Exams from the Start

You are in law school to become a lawyer, not to pass an exam. But to become a lawyer, you do need to pass some exams. At some point in the semester, you will need to take a test displaying all of your knowledge in a course. How are you going to prepare? What is your plan? What source of information will make that studying process helpful? Obviously, you cannot spend the last few days in reading period catching up on everything, so what can you do now? Later? At what moment will you have this accumulation of knowledge completed?

Thinking through these questions early—even at the beginning of the semester—can help you plan. How will you approach outlining? When will you synthesize your notes? When will you practice taking exams? You need answers at the beginning (even if these answers will evolve over time).

The "ask" of 1L year is pretty simple. You will be asked to demonstrate your knowledge on an exam or assessment. This is not a secret. At some point, you are going to have to take the bits and pieces of daily learning and apply this information. You can plan for that moment from the beginning. Don't fool yourself that this should come after everything else. It comes first and should guide your approach to studying, reading, and learning the law.

Books

Buy the Books

Buy the books. Seems simple enough. The professor assigns the books, you buy them. But the temptation is to study on the cheap. Sometimes buying a book that is $200 or more when an older edition is less than half the price is hard to justify.

No matter where you go to school, law school is expensive—too expensive. And the books only add to the expense. While it seems like a place to cut corners, recognize that the information you need to master lies in that text.

Casebooks are like gold—outrageously expensive and intrinsically worthless absent a collective agreement of their value. Yet, like gold, casebooks have survived, mostly out of tradition and because of the manipulated market that law school creates. You could reject these books and the semiprecious analogy on which they are based, or you could treasure them as the collective wisdom of some very smart people that will help you master the material you need to become a lawyer. Acknowledge that you overpaid but then treasure them anyway because of their beauty and educational value.

Read Hornbooks and Treatises

The casebook method of law teaching teaches you to study specific cases in the hope that you will distill the important principles and systemically organize them in your mind. A purist's approach to learning through cases will make the argument that the process of inductive reasoning from case to case is a superior way to learn the law.

Whether or not you choose this method, you should know that there are other methods of understanding a legal subject. In fact, hornbooks and treatises have been written on any subject area you might study. Hornbooks are commercial summaries of the law, organized by subject and issue and helpful for distilling the core principles. Treatises involve academic summaries and commentary of the issues and all of the cases that touch on the legal issue. A complete treatise might dwarf in size your casebook because it attempts to canvass the entire subject on a national scale.

On occasion, try reading hornbooks or treatises on 1L subjects. These books can provide context to the cases. You can see the forest for the trees (as they say) and understand why your professor is so focused on that particular tree. You will understand the history, politics, and rationale and even learn where the law makes no sense. These books cannot replace case reading, but they can augment learning by providing a needed context.

Use Study Aids

In addition to casebooks, hornbooks, and treatises, there exists an entire industry devoted to helping law students understand the law. It is not cheating to read these study aids. You are going to law school to understand the law, so take advantage of these tools.

Books and electronic services exist that correspond to your casebook and can help you master the concepts. Commercial outlines offer examples to shape your own outline. Bar review outlines provide similar material. Case briefs offer shortcut samples of briefs for individual cases. Questions-and-answer books with multiple-choice questions, short-answer questions, and hypotheticals exist for you to test your comprehension. Entire digital empires exist with one goal: to make you understand the law that you are supposed to be learning in law school.

Using these supplemental materials can help. If law school forces you to teach yourself the law, these sources can help guide that education. Of course, they can also provide a crutch so you do not do the other things you need to do to learn. If you only read the case briefs instead of the cases, you will not be learning the law. If you only copy the outlines instead of creating your own, you will not be learning the law. They are helpful tools. But you still have to do your own hard work and know the law. Remember, there will be no commercial outline for being a lawyer. There will be no case brief for a real case. Your future clients deserve more. You are the ultimate product being created by the law school, and you need to be good at your job.

Study the Legal Dictionary

Dictionaries—you might remember them as the things you never used because you could Google the same definition online. The same is true with legal dictionaries, but they are more important.

Imagine going to a country where you could not understand every tenth word. Imagine living in that country permanently. You could, obviously, ignore one-tenth of the substance of what anyone was talking about. Or you could teach yourself the words that you did not understand.

In the olden days, people would read 1L cases with a legal dictionary next to them, looking up every Latin phrase or old-fashioned term of art. They learned the language by looking up definition after definition. What they did not do was remain ignorant or merely skip the words. They taught themselves, and whether in print or online, the point is to learn these old-fashioned legal terms. This is your new language—all lawyers speak it—and you need to become fluent fast.

Law is language. Language is power. And mastering legal language gives you an even greater power. Part of what you are learning in law school is the terms of art of the profession. These words are the key to the secrets of your future, and you need to learn them early.

Find Time for Outside Critical Reading

Lawyers, law professors, judges, journalists, and academics write books and articles on legal issues. Some are even popular. Many offer context, critique, history, and personal narratives around the cases you are reading and the larger issues of the law.

To understand constitutional law, you need to understand US history, and you will not find enough basic history in your casebooks. To understand the structural inequity of race, gender, class, and other forms of discrimination, you need to read the legal analysis of experts who have investigated and exposed the injustices. To understand the political and social currents pushing law's evolution, you need to read about these forces. You get the idea. Read widely and critically. The law needs to be critiqued, and many smart minds have begun the process for you.

You are not bound by the professor's reading assignments. Law school professors provide the minimum, not the maximum, of the available materials. You are teaching yourself, and you will not become a fully educated lawyer by just reading casebooks. For every subject in your class, there are literally hundreds of articles on the subject in law reviews and other publications. You should teach yourself the areas that will enrich your mind (and your career).

Studying

Prepare for Class like an Appellate Argument

Reading for class is not enough. You need to actively prepare. You need to treat each class as an appellate argument. Appellate lawyers argue before appellate judges (usually in panels of three or more) in what is called an "appellate argument." Appellate arguments are formal debates about the particular legal issues raised in an already decided trial court case. Appellate courts decide whether the trial court's legal decisions were correct as a matter of law. Appellate judges ask questions of appellate lawyers not too dissimilar to the questions you get in first-year law classes. The questions are hard, hypothetical, and directed at you.

To succeed, think about class being an appellate argument. Think about the issues ahead of time. Why is this case important? Prepare your argument. What is your response to a question about it? What is the next logical question? What about related issues? You are going into a classroom space where you have to be prepared to keep up. At a minimum, consider:

- If you are asked to recite the facts, what will you say?
- What is the issue that the court decided?
- What is the rule that the court used to decide the case?
- What were the counterarguments?

The only time you will not be scared during an actual court argument is when you have prepared more than anyone else in the room (including the judges). The same is true with class. Preparation equals confidence, which breeds success.

Read Supplements First

Again, you have permission to read supplements (hornbooks, treatises, study aids). A casebook is like a do-it-yourself manual written in lawyer's code, and a supplement is like a real textbook trying to teach you the topic in plain English.

Bearing this is mind, read the supplement first to get a sense of the subject. The supplement will give you a more concrete illustration of the topic or doctrine to be discussed. It is far better to have a more concrete understanding of the topic you are studying first, before you delve into decoding the often complex and verbose vernacular of the judge who wrote the opinion of the case you are studying.

The judge is writing to solve a legal problem. You are reading to understand a legal principle. Focus on the law, reasoning, and rules, not just the results. Remember when reading cases, law matters more than the stories, rules more than the facts. Reading the supplement material first will cause the issues, rules, holdings, and rationales to jump off the pages as you read the cases.

The Secret Structure of Casebooks

Before you even begin reading the cases, study the book itself. By studying the structure of your casebook, you will see the logical framework of how legal issues fit together. You will begin seeing the flow that will allow you to put all of the issues and rules together for analysis.

Generally, each case in a casebook offers an illustration of a particular legal issue. The excerpted text is meant to highlight that issue, with other extraneous material taken out. Focus on seeing the issue and the rules that cover the issue. Look at the table of contents, the structure of the chapter, and then the headings to put the case in context. See how it fits with other cases in the section. Think like the law professor who wrote it. The structure wasn't an accident; figure out the connections.

Casebooks should be read like a collection of short stories, not a novel. Enjoy each case as a stand-alone, well-crafted story. But, like the best collections of short stories, there is a point in the ordering and their internal, hidden connections.

Studying Means Translating

Lawyers are translators, and your classes are your first translation test. The key to being a good translator is to understand the substance yourself in order to translate the content to others. You need to begin finding methods of translation for yourself and others.

Translation is an active process in which you take the concepts and reformulate them in your own head. To understand, you cannot simply read and reread a case. Rereading without interpreting or contextualizing is a waste of time. You need to actively take the concepts and make them make sense to you. After you read a case, imagine a conversation with a nonlawyer friend—a grandmother, sister, or uncle. In this imaginary conversation, explain the case to the person in your own words and describe why the case matters. What are the legal principles at stake? What are the consequences?

You can use supplements or outlines or classmates (or even professors) to help you with that translation process, but the goal is to make the concepts your own. You need to be able to use them, play with them, and explain them to others. Your clients will want to know what the law means, and it will be your job to translate the legal world for them to understand.

Ask "Why" for Each Case

Simple rote memorization of legal rules is not effective. Your ability to excel as a student and future lawyer will depend on your ability to distinguish when those rules apply to a wide range of factual circumstances. To do this, you must know not only the rule but the rationale of the rule—the "why."

As you study rules from cases, you need to try to internalize your understanding of them. A great way to internalize the rules is to learn the "why" of their existence. Why did the judge rule one way or another? What was the driving rationale behind the court's support of such a rule? Ask yourself, "What really motivated the judge to promote the holding?" Analyzing what the judge thought or believed to arrive at legal conclusions helps to embed the rule into your mind. You will not be able to read judges' minds, but you should be able to deduce what was influencing their thinking on the basis of what they wrote in the opinion. Sometimes it is law, policy, text, history, theory, equity, politics, or even ignorance or bias. Once you understand the "why," you will have a deeper understanding of the outcome— even if you disagree with the reasoning or result.

Reading

Read!

Here is an important tip: Read! Read deeply. Read carefully.

Read the cases. Read the notes. You cannot come to class unprepared. You must read (not skim, not blindly highlight, but read) and reread each case. Every hour you practice, you will be improving on a fundamental lawyering skill: critical reading. No matter what kind of lawyer you become, you will be reading every day of your career.

Every day in law school, you need to set aside several hours for reading. If you find yourself routinely reading in the moments just before class, you are doing it wrong. Reading the cases is a necessary but not sufficient condition for success. It is necessary—you need to know what the case says. But it is not sufficient to master the material. You need to have time to think about the case, outline the case, and process the case in the context of the entire class.

Read on Three Levels

Class reading requires you to read on three levels:

Level 1: Read for the who, what, where, and why. You need to be able to tell the story in a narrative fashion. "What are the facts" means "tell me the story of the case."

Level 2: Think about fit. How does the case fit within the class, the course, the subject? What is the central reason you are reading this case, and how does it fit within other reading assignments? What is the legal issue that this case explains?

Level 3: What is my takeaway from the case? How will I use the rule, remember it, apply it? What are the rules I can apply for the next case? Why does it matter? What proposition does the case stand for?

Distilling the facts, issues, and rules in the case are the key goals of critical, active reading. This may be a different way than you usually read. We think of reading as an internal pursuit. But when you are reading for class, you are reading to do something with the material. You are going to make external use of this reading material in class, in an argument, or on an exam.

Find the "Takeaway" of Each Case

As you read a case, it is important to have a process to gain the most from your reading. You will instinctively recognize "what" has happened in a set of facts, but it is more important for you to know "why" the case is in the casebook.

There are thousands of cases one could put in a casebook to provide a representative example of a crime, a contract, a tort, or a civil procedure dispute. So why did the author pick this case? It was not just to entertain you. What is the reason why this case helps to explain the law?

If you can find the point of the case—why this case was included in the book to explain a particular point—you will see the important takeaway of the reading. Most cases can be distilled down to one point, one rule, one argument that justifies its inclusion in the book.

Remember, while all the facts, arguments, analysis, and filler will be fodder for classroom discussion and debate, the case is included to add one (maybe two or three) legal principles to your growing legal knowledge.

Read the Footnotes, the Concurring Opinions, and the Dissents

Those pesky footnotes and long dissents are often overlooked by many overwhelmed 1Ls. As you grind through page after page, you just want to get your reading assignment over with before class. But there is value in those footnotes and dissents, and skipping them will be costly. The footnotes offer enlightenment on the nuances of the rule being analyzed in the case. Your professor will almost definitely ask about those nuances in class and maybe on your final exam.

When you read a case without reading all of the opinions (concurrences and dissents), you miss a helpful example of how rules can be interpreted differently. The dissents often point out flaws in the majority opinion's reasoning (sometimes using the very same rules). In addition, the concurring opinions often highlight additional perspectives and rationales for the current holding.

If you study how judges craft arguments using the same facts and rules but come to different outcomes, you will see how to do it as an advocate.

Simplify Sentences as You Read

The sentence structure in cases is often confusing. Judges use complex words and phrases. To combat this confusion, simplify the sentence by rephrasing it into your own words.

Rewrite the ideas in your own words. As they say, "Write, don't highlight." Most of the rules you will learn can be distilled down to an "if-then" statement of logic. Adding an exception becomes an "if-then-unless" statement. Deconstructing the rules so you can understand them will make it easier for you to memorize and apply them in an exam.

Take the time to write out important rules. Words matter, and you cannot merely substitute your preferred words for the judge's legal terminology; but you can make it understandable. Find a way to make a precise, concise, and complete definition of the rule. This rule will end up in your brief of the case, in your outline, and on the exam. Make it yours.

Briefing Cases

Briefing Means Decoding and Encoding

During the first week, you will brief every case and promise yourself you will continue to do so all semester. By the second week, you will start taking shortcuts, using commercial case briefs, or just underlining extra hard. This is a common but counterproductive approach. Do the hard work of briefing your own cases.

Briefing cases matters because the briefing process forces you to deconstruct the structure of a case. By breaking down the facts, pulling out the issues, rewriting the rules, and mastering the holding, you are decoding how the law is put together, while at the same time encoding it as your own.

If you merely copy the words on the page, you are doing it wrong. Briefing involves active learning. The repetitive process of breaking down cases and building up your own knowledge is central to being a good lawyer. You are building the muscle memory of legal reasoning, and it takes repetition, thought, and practice. The goal is that after doing this for a year, the ability to break down and organize a case will be intuitive. You will never have to think twice in your career if you can master this skill now. After a year, the skill will be in your lawyerly DNA.

Train Your Mind—See the IRAC Pattern

In time, you will sense that IRAC (issue, rule, analysis, conclusion) is the secret key to success on law school exams. On an issue-spotting exam, there are issues for you to spot. Each issue has a rule. Each rule can be applied to the facts. This application is the analysis. The analysis leads to a conclusion. Writing an answer in IRAC format (or some variant) will become a constant drumbeat as you hear about ways to succeed on exams.

But if you study your briefed cases, you will also see the IRAC pattern. Judges routinely start cases with sentences like, "The issue in this case is . . ." and methodically list out the elements of the rule. The rule is then analyzed against the facts, providing the analysis and then the conclusion.

If you start seeing that many cases follow the IRAC pattern and many legal arguments follow the IRAC pattern, you will see why the framework is also so useful on exams.

Every 1L course teaches you a variety of issues. Again, each issue has a rule. Your task on an exam (or in life) is to identify the issue, cite the rule, apply the facts, and come up with a conclusion. Judges do that every day in their written opinions. Litigators do it in their briefs. Lawyers do it every day in solving problems. It is the pattern that links all your class work and the work you will do as a lawyer.

"Frame Out" Your Cases

Comprehending all the information in a case is difficult. Summarizing cases is even more difficult. There are a lot of moving parts to synthesize as you read. Some 1Ls say that they read a case only to feel as though they didn't "get it." They then try to read it a second time, and some even read it a third time to understand what is going on.

Before you jump into reading a case, identify and mark the structure of the text first. Diving in first without analyzing the flow of the reading will slow down your comprehension and memory of the whole picture. Think of the case as a series of sections connected for a common purpose: to articulate a rule and then a legal result from that rule.

A memorable way to think of this process is to "frame out" before you "drain out" the contents of a case. To accomplish this, (1) identify the beginning and end of the factual statement, (2) identify the procedural posture, (3) identify the question for the court to decide, (4) identify the law (rule) used to decide the case, (5) identify the court's application of the law, and (6) identify the holding. Create the frame for your own understanding.

This may seem like it will take longer, but it actually speeds up your reading because you don't find yourself rereading the same text over and over. You will come to appreciate being able to take in a case through manageable chunks of information instead of wading through page after page and wondering what is really being said.

RULE 29

Use Briefs as a Self-Test

The brief is your take on a case. Use it as a moment to self-test your knowledge about the issues that arise from the case.

Most students see briefing as a preparation tool for class, a security blanket for when the professor calls on you to give the correct facts, issue, rule, analysis, and so on. But briefs can also be used to test yourself before class. At the end of every brief, write down in your own words what the point of this case is and the rule. Test yourself to see if you can operationalize why the case is important and what the takeaway should be from the case. And after class, go back and see if you were correct.

These case briefs will also provide the source material for your outlines and studying. There is no way to reread the entire semester's worth of cases to prepare for exams, so you will default to your case briefs. These summaries will be the way you think about the cases, and thus crafting them precisely, thoroughly, and accurately is terribly important. If you misstate something in your brief, you might end up misunderstanding the law.

Briefing for Context

Briefing cases involves more than understanding the facts and law. Build a habit of looking at the law from a historical perspective. Understand its context. What year was it written? In what court? By what judge or justice?

Doing this will further strengthen your ability to internalize the law. Knowing where a law came from gives a perspective and understanding of what the law was meant to do. Knowing who wrote the opinion can provide context.

Law is a reflection of social power and social norms. To understand the law is to see how these forces shape the outcome. Politics, legal philosophy, and history shape the law, and these influences should be included in your case summaries. When you learn about the history of a law, you can visually map out the progression of the law and its effect on social conditions and other outcomes. You can see the development of the law (for good or bad) through your notes.

In Class

Class Is like Oral Argument

Law school classes are discomfiting experiences. They tend to be large and fast-paced, with sharp and pointed questions. Professors call on students and demand a response. To prepare for this experience, it helps actually to be prepared. At a minimum, you can prepare for questions about the facts, the issue, the rule, the holding, the procedural posture, and your own evaluation of the strength of the court's argument. If you follow through on briefing cases, you will be 70 percent of the way prepared for any question.

The harder questions in class involve hypotheticals that make you apply the rules to other scenarios or ask you to argue on one side or the other. These questions can also be thought through and prepared before class. Although you may not know the direction of a particular class discussion, the questions arising from application of the rules can be considered ahead of time.

That process of guessing the next problem, identifying the logical consequences, or seeing the traps of an argument is part of the skill set you are mastering. The facts will change, but the rules will remain the same. This is the skill of an oral advocate. Class is a mini oral argument on a few discrete cases and issues. And while this skill is not natural to most people, it can be learned, practiced, and developed.

RULE 32

Ban Your Own Laptop

We live and learn in a hyperconnected age. At any moment, there could be a social media update or news event. Our addiction to staying digitally engaged makes taking notes on a laptop in class quite difficult. While you may think you can focus on the professor while emailing, updating your social media accounts, and shopping online, in truth you cannot. Studies show that students who are forced to take handwritten notes in class have better recall of the material and are more engaged. By tuning out the distractions of life, students can focus on the questions in class.

Consider banning your own laptop or at a minimum forcing yourself to stop multitasking. There will be no social media or email during the final exam, so train your brain to focus. If you must use a computer in class, ban email, ban instant communications, ban the internet, and ban social media during class time. You will not miss anything important, and you will gain a level of deep focus necessary to master the law.

Notes Should Be Reflection, Not Transcription

Taking class notes is an exercise in reflection, not transcription. You need to be actively thinking about engaging in the ideas, not simply writing down the words or copying down the slides of your professor.

Your task is to distill the ideas, issues, rules, and debates into usable frameworks for analysis. When you go back to review those notes after class or before the exam, a transcript will be less helpful than a few key points about the issues discussed, the rules, and any elements of those rules that can be applied to future cases.

Class notes are poetry, not prose.

Just as reading for class is not an internal pursuit, neither is note-taking. You are not taking notes to keep the ideas hidden for yourself; you are taking notes to be able to apply them in the future. The goal is to find the core rules that will be applied later, in class, in a conversation, or on an exam.

Engage, Don't Hide

Your professor can see you. You might think you can hide in a large 1L classroom. You might think you can avoid being judged. But you cannot. Professors are watching you, your reaction, your eyes. They can see you yawn, smile at an email, or try to avoid answering a question. They can see whether you choose to engage or hide.

Teachers see everything and evaluate accordingly. If you step back and think about what teachers are doing in class, all they are doing is talking and watching. It is not hard to do both, so be warned that what you think is a sly look about a funny message is completely registered by the professor teaching the class.

A law professor sees two types of students in class. One type of student actively listens, makes eye contact, asks questions, writes down the important points, and processes the material. The other type of student sits facing a computer, half processing, head down, avoiding the conversation and the learning process. Whether you like it or not, you are being judged, so be the active learner, not the passive avoider.

Appreciate Teaching-Style Federalism

Each professor teaches in a different way, and this creates a sense of inconsistency for students trying to understand "the law." But this difference is actually a strength, not a weakness, of the law school method.

The strength of federalism in the United States is that states can create different laws than the federal government. States can experiment, respond to local issues, or be mini laboratories of democracy. While the differing rules can be frustrating to anyone trying to understand them, they also reflect the reality that there is no "one" way to organize government. So it is with law school classes taught by different professors. Like the diversity of states, law professors teach with different styles, with different approaches, and with different expectations. While the differing rules can be frustrating, they reflect the reality that there is no one way to learn the law.

As a lawyer, you need to master your state's laws. It will do you no good to be an expert on some other state's laws. The same is true with judges. You will know what your judges like, what they respond to, and how to craft an argument. Each one is different, and it takes study to understand the best strategy to succeed. Similarly, with law school, you need to master the local rules of your law school. Each professor does things slightly differently, and that is okay. Instead of being frustrated, just realize that it is another thing to learn, the mastery of which will help you succeed as a lawyer.

IN CLASS | 65

Habits of Success

Undergraduate Study Habits Must Die

The skills that allowed you to survive your undergraduate education no longer work in law school. Accept the difference. Do not fight it. No more all-nighters. No cramming. No winging it. There is too much to learn at too precise a level of detail. Pre-law-school life habits must die, or your GPA will.

While there are superficial similarities to past educational pursuits, law school is a fundamentally different educational experience, and you must recalibrate accordingly. The workload, reading, assignments, level of precision, speed, and expectations simply exceed the demands of even the best undergraduate schools. Everyone works hard in law school, and the pressures ramp up.

Study habits must evolve to adjust to this new reality. Treat law school like a full-time job. Get up early. Stay late. Work throughout the day, and you will find time for other things. Law school is a job in itself, and you need to build study habits accordingly.

Checklist Each Day

Law school semesters are overpacked. Each day is valuable, even if just to decompress. You need to organize the chaos. The revolving deadlines, obligations, and accumulated assignments can catch up with you. Just daily reading can take up all your free time. Two hours of self-study for each class hour are the minimum, and they add up.

There always will be other things to accomplish: summer job applications, community service, student activities, and so on. Plus studying and taking practice exams. To balance the ever-increasing responsibilities, each day should be planned out with small and achievable accomplishments. Use checklists.

Every day brings a new checklist of things to do. Plan to outline two pages. Reread one case, or remove one future obligation from your to-do list. Checklists give you control.

Find Solitude to Study

Your study location must provide solitude. No matter your learning style, you need time alone to input the information. Finding solitude is best done by finding a place away from other law students. Every interruption while you are reading breaks your focus. Each time that happens, you will lose some of what you have understood due to the fragmentation of the information.

You may like the concept of studying in groups, but until you have your own process of understanding the materials for yourself, you will not be of any use in a group study with your peers. Being in a group environment without having a basic understanding of the materials will only frustrate you and your study partners. Study groups work, but only after you have studied yourself.

Law students are not your only problem. Family, friends, and coffee-shop patrons also will infringe on your solitude. If you try to work in a place where others can reach you, you will lose valuable time. Find a place where you can retreat, read, and reflect. Guard that space, defend your isolation.

Ignore Social Media

Reading, thinking, and applying the law can be hard, dare we say, boring. The temptations of our hyperconnected, ever-changing world can cause you to lose focus while studying.

Law school was designed in a pre-digital age and hasn't quite adapted. Reading books is old-fashioned. Writing long legal briefs is old-fashioned. Arguing before a judge is old-fashioned. But even in our current digital era, those traditional skills are necessary. You must develop the skills to thrive in that pre-digital world because many of the senior lawyers and judges still live there.

Turn off the social media world when you study. Put your smartphone away. Ignore the next update by a friend. Shut out everything but the law. Your phone and digital life are addictive. You must find a way to remove yourself from those distractions. At least during your studying time, you need to focus on only one thing. Make studying and class a distraction-free time.

Prioritize Time Management

Time management may be the single biggest reason people underperform in law school. Students do not leave enough time to study, to outline, to take practice exams, or even to take the actual exam. Understanding how much time it will take you to accomplish a task, master a skill, or prepare for an exam is something many people learn the hard way. They fail.

Focusing on time management at the beginning can make all the difference in the end. You should create calendars and charts of your days, weeks, months, and the time you will spend doing the tasks at hand. You should time yourself taking practice exams to see how long it takes you to write out an answer. You should block out more time than you need to rewrite legal writing assignments.

At the beginning of every week, you should block out the time you will be studying, reading, outlining, or completing other assignments. Study how long it takes you and adapt. Everything will take longer than you think, so plan your time accordingly.

Confidence

Get Your Mind Right

Before any challenge in law school, you need to deal with mental impediments to success. All the negative thoughts, most of the fear, and every self-doubting echo in your head must be silenced before you can move on to your activity. Self-doubt leads to self-sabotage, and many great students stop themselves before they can begin.

In writing this book, we asked lots of lawyers how they experienced the first weeks of law school. All said they had no idea what they were doing. Top students, brilliant lawyers, and some of the most truly impressive people all agreed that 1L year is baffling, humbling, and not easy. Remember, no one comes to law school fully prepared. Even your most confident classmates have no idea what they are doing. They are bluffing. But they have their minds right. So get yours right too.

You Belong in Law School

Understand that you are fully capable and ready to undertake the challenge ahead of you. Regardless of your past failings and the current immensity of the work ahead, you will survive law school.

Your adaptation to this new environment depends on your understanding of yourself, your habits, and the way law school really works. But remember, you wouldn't be occupying one of almost forty thousand seats at an ABA-accredited law school in the United States if someone in power (and with experience) didn't think you were capable and ready for this. You have grit and creativity, and you know how to struggle, which are all positive skills for law school.

Anyone who walks through the door as a 1L can graduate and pass the bar exam with enough work and dedication. Remember:

- The best lawyers are not the smartest but those who work the hardest.
- The best lawyers are not the quickest but those who think the deepest.
- The best lawyers are not the most pedigreed but those who are the most prepared.

Accept the Learning Curve

Just like in any new endeavor, whether it's running a business or riding a bike, you should expect there to be a learning curve or time period before you really understand what is going on. Becoming a law student is no different.

You should expect that it is most probable that you will not do everything right the first time out of the gate in law school. However, failing until you get it right is part of the learning process. Own it and expect this. Don't beat yourself up when you miss a small detail in a fact pattern or forget an argument in a case. Even if you flop big by failing a class, remember that you can master the material with enough work.

Some students will take longer to get it. The point is to expect mistakes and not to feel like you are slow or deficient in learning the process because of them. It's your learning process, and your steps to becoming a successful law student may be at a different tempo than others'.

Law's Disorienting Effect

Law school can be a disempowering experience. In addition to the workload, the stress, and the challenge of learning new and difficult material, you must face the reality that the law perpetuates inequality.

For much of history, law was written by white men of power deciding the fates of women, people of color, and the poor, while maintaining power and property for themselves. Case outcomes are unfair, cruel, and biased and yet can be perfectly legal. For students who see (and feel) the injustice of the outcomes, law school can be a disorienting and dispiriting time. What is the role of a lawyer in a system that perpetuates inequality and injustice? What does it say when the law ignores the powerless or voiceless? Recognize that only those who can see the injustice in law will be able to change it. It is absolutely critical for law students to question, challenge, and improve the system of structural power that we call the law.

Lift Others Up

The adversarial nature of law can create negative pressures to denigrate others. You are learning to be competitive. You are learning to beat others in argument. And the results can be unkind.

In addition, the power dynamics and social inequality outside law school can find their way into law school classes. Insider and outsider, rich and poor, left and right, and all the other differences can make their way into class discussions.

Don't be that person who puts others down to feel good. Be that person who lifts others up so all can succeed. Don't be that person who divides. Be the person who unites. Comport yourself in a civil and professional manner, and open your mind and heart to those who see the world differently.

The best law school classes are like a close family. You will share way too much with this group. You will see births, death, love, and hate in your time as a law school family. Recognize that like a healthy family, you need to generate support for others. You need to care for others. You have a responsibility to lift others up.

If you are lucky, you will befriend a person who is completely different from you, who sees the world in a completely different light, and yet becomes a professional ally for the rest of your life.

Outlines

Distill, Distill, Distill

Outlines are critical to mastering a subject. Outlines are the distilled points of a course broken down by issue and rule. A good outline provides a visual framework for how the issues in a class should be organized. Large topic areas are subject headings. Relevant issues fall below those topics. Rules are broken down by elements for analysis to follow the issues.

1. Issue
2. Rule statement and elements of rule
3. Cases and facts to remember
4. Exceptions

An outline is not a series of case briefs. An outline is not a repetition of class notes. An outline is a distillation of core points that can be applied to an exam question or legal problem. Find an example of an outline for your course. Read it, and then draft your own.

Begin Outlining Immediately

Outlining involves distilling ideas, so it is hard to begin outlining before you see how the issues fit together. For this reason, people suggest waiting to outline. This is good advice for some students and bad for others.

Those who counsel waiting are absolutely correct that a good outline involves being able to see what matters with regard to issues and rules. At the beginning, everything seems important, so everything gets included. Of course, an outline that includes everything is not an outline. But for many students, the waiting approach means waiting until it's too late. If you wait until midterms, too much material has been covered. Worse, class readings will not stop, and writing assignments will increase; plus you have to study for midterms (and finals).

The hardest part of outlining is just starting. Once you start, you will see that the material just fills in itself. But you have to start setting up the framework to fill in. If you get behind, you really get behind. So if you begin early, even with just a limited, not-so-good outline, it becomes much easier to fill in the gaps. It becomes much easier to keep up with the material. Start early, and do a bit every day you can.

Collaborate on Outlines

Outlining need not be a solitary project. Every student in your class is learning the same material and going through the same process. Every 1L student across the country is essentially learning the same subject. Every year the same wheel gets invented.

Sharing outlines, borrowing outlines from 2Ls or 3Ls, and comparing your outline to commercial outlines are all positive and acceptable things to do. There is no one way to outline or organize the material in a class, and you should see different versions.

More importantly, you do not need to reinvent the wheel of contracts or torts or criminal law. The "black-letter law" is the same and has been the same for years. You need to understand it, and if collaborating with others will help you, then do it.

A Mind Map

No matter how you create your outline, it should do one thing for you: it should create a mind map of a subject. A mind map allows you to see the organizational structure of a subject—for example, how criminal defenses apply to elements of criminal offenses or how "acceptance" is related to an "offer" in a valid contract.

The key to a mind map is flow. Some maps are horizontal, so the entire class spreads out with decision trees of issues, elements, and possible analytical choices. Some maps are vertical, with subjects listed by issue in more traditional outline form. Others are almost artistic, with a host of circle diagrams and arrows and textboxes. Whatever way you choose, you must "see" the totality of a class and connect the different issues together.

Mind maps are important not only for spotting issues and defining rules but also for seeing the organizing structure of the class so that your exam answers will flow from this structure.

The Front Page

Your outline may be long or short. Some are ten pages, some are sixty. The outline may cover every single word of your notes or be a distilled version of the rules. But at the front of every outline should be a one-page summary sheet.

Think of this front page as the table of contents to your outline, or perhaps the outline of your outline. This front page should be the distilled organization of the class material. This is also your issue-spotting guide. This one page will be the key to whether you can see all the issues in a class jump out from the page. If the secret to exam taking (and lawyering) is issue-spotting in a quick and logical manner, then this is the secret to the secret.

If you have outlined correctly and if your outline created a mind map, you will probably not ever need to refer to anything besides this first page. It will guide you through the issue-spotting and trigger your rules and answers.

Application,
Application,
Application

Test Yourself

If you simply read and reread the cases assigned, you are likely to do poorly in law school. Reading is not the same thing as applying the law. You have to find ways to test yourself. If you simply memorize the rules, you will think you know the law, but you will only be half ready for an exam. You need to test those rules on new facts.

Find supplements, tests, or quizzes and force yourself to apply the rules you have learned from the cases. You will see that reading provides only the basic knowledge, with none of the nuance you need to master the course.

Only by testing (and getting the answers wrong until you get them right) will you start to see the level of detail needed to master the course. Application, application, application is really repetition, repetition, repetition, and the key to success. This cannot be emphasized enough. Application means taking practice exams, studying practice exams, and taking them again. Application means challenging yourself to fail in your first few attempts. Application means testing yourself so hard that the final exam seems routine. There is no substitute. There is no other way.

Find Hypotheticals in Life

There is a reason your professor uses hypotheticals to teach. Hypotheticals force you to apply your knowledge. Class would be pretty boring if all anyone did was recite the facts that everyone else had already read.

Hypotheticals are about applying rules to new facts. And you do not have to wait until class to get into the game. You can find other hypothetical questions in books and supplements. You can create your own. You can annoy your friends with creative examples. You can imagine how a rule might apply to a slightly different situation.

If you can see how your rule applies to the next hypothetical, you will be ready to apply your knowledge on an exam—which is, after all, just another hypothetical.

But this skill goes beyond the test. You need to be prepared for the day when a client walks into your office and tells you a story. The story will be about their legal troubles, and your job will be to spot the legal issues that you can help them with. The skill of issue spotting from a hypothetical story becomes all too real when that client looks into your eyes and asks for legal help. The same process of looking at the facts, spotting how the law interacts with the facts, and then thinking about the consequences of that legal analysis is the skill of lawyering.

Mastery Requires Repetitive, Iterative Practice

Human beings do not learn anything without practice. This includes law students. Our brains retain information most effectively when we see the information again and again. We need to find the patterns. Law is filled with patterns.

Law school should be understood as an iterative learning process, in which you build up your knowledge bit by bit, relearning, and repeating what you know by putting it in context for better comprehension. The daily tasks of briefing, note-taking, and outlining are designed to mirror this repetitive, iterative process of learning.

But you also need to review the material yourself. If you only look at your notes after the course has ended and try to remember everything over the past three months, you are doing yourself a disservice. Review every week (if not every day). Build in a practice of skimming through your notes and case briefs to remind yourself from where you started. You will see the patterns emerge. You will see the connections link together. You will see the intersections with other classes. The patterns in the law repeat. The patterns of learning repeat. Start looking for patterns.

See the Connecting Thread

1L year feels fragmented. You are learning different sub-jects. You have different professors. Each one seems to have a different style or method. In your head, you focus on the particular demands of particular classes, but remember that there is a thread running through these experiences—they are all asking you to do the same thing: spot the issues, identify the rules, analyze the law, and give your legal opinion.

In a year or so, you will look back on 1L classes and realize that they were not all that different, that you were learning the same thing just through different means. You will see that the focus on mastering different substantive classes masked the similarities of the approach. The basic skill set is transferrable to any other class.

In a few short years, you will have mastered other sub-jects, worked in clinics, helped clients, passed the bar exam, and started your professional life. 1L year will be a blur. But there will be a connecting thread through all of these experiences. Each one will require you to apply the law. The facts will change. The law will be different. The law you will be applying may not even exist now. But when you are asked to use your lawyering skills, it will be about doing the very thing you are learning right now. You will see that what you learned is not just a subject but a way of thinking and problem-solving.

RULE 55

If There Is an Answer, They Don't Need
to Hire a Lawyer

The simple reason to focus on applying the law, rather than memorizing the law, is that, in application, lawyers show their value. Despite the term "black-letter law," in truth the law is gray, blurry, and sometimes a rainbow of contrasting shades. Almost every case has at least two sides and more than two possible outcomes. Lawyers take from what is fixed or settled in the law and then apply those principles to the question at hand. If there already was an obvious answer, no one would hire a lawyer. But there rarely is an easy answer, which is why lawyers must apply the law to the facts at hand.

When you pick up a casebook, "creativity" might not be your first thought, but lawyers have creatively shaped the law through argument. Every argument, distinguishing factor, analogy, and historical fact has helped literally to "create" the law. Law is a living organism that is created and re-created every day by lawyers applying the law.

The biggest takeaway for 1L year is that you must be able to apply legal rules to the next problem. That's your value.

Legal Writing/ Research

Pay Attention in Legal Research Class

Among many overworked 1L students, there will often be a strong inclination to diminish the importance of your legal research class. Resist this urge. The skills gleaned from a legal research class are among the most important and widely used skills you will possess as a law student and lawyer.

One day, you are going to be sitting in your office, and a client is going to approach you with a legal question. You will not know the answer. It will not have been covered in a law school class. There will not be a textbook directly on point. But the client needs an answer. You must be able to conduct legal research about an area of law that you know nothing about. You must be able to find, digest, distill, and apply that law on behalf of a client. You must be able to research new areas of law.

Throughout your entire legal career, your ability to find the applicable law, properly state it, and cite to it will be used over and over again. Legal research class will hone that set of skills. If you fail to grasp this skill, you will unnecessarily waste valuable research time. Moreover, you will handicap yourself going into your second-year classes.

The skills learned in legal research are foundational, and the importance of participating wholeheartedly in these classes cannot be stressed enough. Every single day in law school and after law school, you will be a legal researcher.

You Cannot Write

You think you can write. Sure, you have been writing your whole life. Sure, legal writing seems just like normal writing and should be easy. You are wrong.

Legal writing is not more difficult than other types of writing. It is not more complicated. But it is different, and that difference must be understood and accepted.

Once you accept this truth, you will also accept the constructive criticism coming from your legal writing professors. Be kind. Legal writing professors have the hardest jobs on the faculty because they must tell you to improve your writing to your face (not hidden behind blind grading rules). No one wants to hear they could do better, especially at something as personal as writing, but you should listen to the hard truths your professors share.

Once you accept these truths, you will start to see the structure, form, language, and conventions that distinguish legal work. You will distinguish between legal writing as advocacy and legal writing as advice. You will see the style of judicial opinions as opposed to legal scholarship. You will see that lawyers write a lot and that plenty of examples exist.

Once you accept the truth that you cannot write, you can start studying the craft of legal writing. No one is born a great legal writer. It takes work, study, practice, and editing.

Proofread for Precision and Perfection

There are remarkably few typographical errors in published legal writing. And when an error is spotted, it becomes a big deal. When a Supreme Court justice misspells a word, it becomes a national news story. Law review articles—the kind your law professors write for a living—are usually edited dozens of times even after the final (supposedly perfect) draft is submitted. A single misplaced comma or typographical error is grounds for shame. The audience that will read your written work expects perfection in spelling, grammar, and logical structure.

1L year is a time to develop your proofreading skills. Any final paper should go through multiple drafts. Read your writing aloud. Read it backward, sentence by sentence (to break up the flow). Read it for structure and transitions. Spell-check.

Do not send anything to anyone without proofreading for precision and perfection—not even an email or informal note. This is a fundamental rule—again, do not ever send anything to anyone without proofreading for precision and perfection. You will be judged, dismissed, and not taken seriously if any error makes it into the final product.

Mistakes will happen, but proofreading for precision and perfection is the norm of legal writing. Professional lawyers are perfectionists, and you must become one.

See Infra the Importance of Citations

Citations play an outsized role in legal writing. Legal citations provide the reader the ability to see what sources of information support the legal claim and where to find them. Citations create a shared language to understand the basis of the argument and thus why it might be a more convincing claim.

Almost every opinion, brief, or legal document consists primarily of an argument and the citations that support those arguments. Both argument and citation are necessary. In law, as opposed to other fields, arguments without citations lack strength.

Citations can be in footnotes, in endnotes, or in the text. Most legal citations follow the *Bluebook* format, which is one possible way to cite a source. The *Bluebook* provides a way to standardize the information that would be necessary to find the source. Other citation systems include the *Maroon Book*, created by the *University of Chicago Law Review*, and the *ALWD Guide to Legal Citation*, created by the Association of Legal Writing Directors.

Learning how to cite and figuring out its importance can be wonderfully helpful to you. You can save time and energy if you know what the conventions involve. Learn it early. Learn it once. And you can keep the skill for the rest of your career.

Law Librarians Are Wizards

Imagine there was a person at the law school who knew where all the information about a particular subject was kept and who had the job to tell you. Would that person be the first person or the last person you asked for help?

Law librarians are like the wizards of the legal profession. They collect and curate vast stores of knowledge and magically make them appear when asked. Most academic law librarians hold law degrees and master's degrees in information science. They know not only more than you do but also how to find even more information. If you think about your textbooks as the first volume of a warehouse of written materials on each legal subject, you will see the need for someone to find the most relevant materials among the stacks.

If your task is to find out information about a particular legal subject (which is the job of a lawyer), you should take advantage of a librarian's magic. And then stick around for some lessons on how to become a research wizard yourself.

Professors

Meet with Your Professor

Professors get paid a decent wage to teach you the law. So get your money's worth and go talk to them. Many are quite nice. Some are wonderful. And you will eventually need a letter of recommendation, a door opened, or some career advice, so it makes sense for them to know you as a fully formed person (not a hand raised in a large class).

Professors who teach 1L courses love 1Ls. There is a special joy in teaching students as they first learn the law. These professors want to meet with you, learn from you, and help you understand the material. They really do.

Professors also have lots of students over the years and far too many professional commitments (teaching, scholarship, service, life), and they can come across as too busy for students. But professors are teachers first, and all of them (even the grumpy, self-absorbed ones) will warm up to your questions, insights, and concerns if you show up (with an appointment) at their office.

Professors can help you find perspective during the crush of exams, provide substantive answers on confusing questions of law, and even occasionally find you a job. Be respectful, be engaged, and make an effort to be seen by them in person. Knowing your professor is an important part of law school, and one you should not forsake.

To Impress, Engage the Law

Professors routinely have to write recommendations for students, forcing them to think about what makes a good student. In a class of one hundred or more students who all read the same material and who all more or less answered the questions, how can anyone stand out? What would make a student stand out?

The answer is engagement. The best students are those who are excited by the law, curious about its intricacies, and inspired by the process of learning. It is not about grades or background or charm. Those students who tend to shine are those who are not simply prepared but engaged in the process of discovering the law.

How do you show engagement? Ask questions. Think hard about the implications of the legal rules. Question the doctrine. Read outside the textbook. Think about it this way: your professors have devoted their professional careers to a particular area of the law. They think about the issues all the time. For whatever reason, they find it fascinating. Any student who chooses to think about these issues and talk to professors about what they love is going to be well received and well regarded. To you, it is just a class. To your professors, it is their life's work.

Understand What Law Professors Really Do

You see a professor as a teacher, who teaches a few times a week, who grades exams (slowly), who holds office hours. But teaching is just one of the things professors do. Most law professors must also write scholarly articles to keep their job. This involves research, writing, editing, and thought. Many write books, conduct empirical studies, or help clients.

Most law professors are also experts in some field and are called to help others with that knowledge. Law professors routinely travel to trainings, conferences, and trials and speak to journalists and government agencies interested in their ideas. In addition, in order to improve their articles and ideas, law professors travel to debate and discuss their ideas at other schools. All of this work is part of the "scholarship" requirements of the job.

But there is more. Law professors also run the school through committees on curricular development, faculty appointments, admissions, academic support, and general administration. They are also responsible for evaluating fellow professors, advising student groups, and supervising independent studies.

This is part of the "service" requirement of being a law professor. Law professors are evaluated not only on teaching but also on scholarship and service, so when they are not in front of you doing the former, they are probably doing the latter.

Understand Your Professors' Interests

Professors are scholars and advocates and are engaged in the life of the law in some way. As is natural, these interests infuse and inform their teaching. As students, you can get a competitive advantage in class if you understand your professor's research and work interests.

Many times, if you want to understand an issue or a question of law or wonder why professors are emphasizing a particular point, it is because they are interested in that issue. They might have written an article on the subject. They might be the national expert. You can understand their approach to law if you understand their scholarship or advocacy. Almost every law professor has a track record of writing about the very subjects you are studying. If you read their articles (most free and available, even if long and overly footnoted), you will get insights into their ideas and views.

Just as you might research the judge hearing your case or an opponent in litigation to gain a competitive advantage, you should research your professors to understand how they think, work, and view the law.

Professors Do Not Represent the Law

Diversity in law school faculties is improving but is not close to perfect. Unfortunately, there is a gender and racial gap in who teaches at law schools in the United States. Worse, the primary people who have been teaching about the law over the past century have been white men. Not surprisingly, the interests and views of powerful white men have been disproportionately taught. This can create a representation problem in the law.

Remember that professors do not represent the law. Your presence in law school and your interpretation of the law are just as valid as any professor's. Your perspective and critiques will improve the law. When you graduate, you will be a lawyer just like your professor, and your views will hold equal weight in court, in practice, in articles, or anywhere else.

Representation matters. In classes, on panels, in lectures, the people the law school asks to represent the legal profession matter. As a member of your law school community, it is your responsibility to remind people that representation matters. Students pick their own leaders. Students pick speakers. Students organize panels. Students select "professors of the year." Each of the choices of whom to showcase reflects a choice about representation, and representation matters.

Extracurricular
Activities

Motivate Yourself with Idealism

Many law students come to law school to make a differ-ence. Being in law school actually allows you to make that difference. You can use the law. You can volunteer. You can work in clinics. It is exciting, seductive, and far more engaging than reading a casebook for class.

Do not ever lose your idealism, and use it to motivate yourself to study. The reason you are learning these skills is to help others—others who will rely on you to help them navigate the legal system. Use your idealism to fuel the fire of long nights, hard work, and a bit more reading.

Here is the truth about lawyering on behalf of other people, especially those without power: it's hard. It's hard because the law is written for the powerful. It's hard be-cause there are few resources. It's hard because legal practice is tough even in the best of situations. But those people now depend on you—the same you who has a choice about how you want to approach law school. You can approach law school to get the most out of it or just get by. You can approach your legal education with seriousness or not. And while it might not matter all that much to you at the end of the day, it certainly will matter to your clients.

Focus on Law-Related Projects

As you explore the world of work outside the law school, make sure you focus on law-related projects. The double education of learning through a legal project can make abstract principles come alive. Find jobs related to law. Learn about clerkships or professional associations like the ABA. Meet judges and learn about what lawyers actually do from lawyers themselves.

Lots of jobs exist for law students during law school. The reason: you are free labor (and smart free labor at that). Many nonlegal community organizations need legal help but, like the rest of us, cannot afford to hire an attorney. Law students can help fill that gap, and you can be given many wonderful opportunities. But it is even more valuable to work with lawyers (even in the same spaces). Observing how practicing lawyers problem-solve, negotiate, investigate, and litigate will put the entire law school experience in perspective. You will see how the cases you read about come alive in court. You will see the human dimension of lawyering (and that most success comes from that human dimension). You offer a valuable service with your time and labor. Gain your own benefit by watching legal professionals do the job you are training to do.

Extracurricular Internships Do Not Track Law School Time-Lines

The law school semester has a definite time-line. The real world does not always track that time-line. One of the challenges in volunteering for extracurricular responsibilities during your 1L year is that sometimes these two time-lines collide.

Unquestionably, working for legal organizations during the first year of law school can be life-changing. But, not infrequently, the demands of the real-world client or employer will not line up neatly with your study schedule. This conflict can cause you to ignore your extracurricular commitments to the detriment of your reputation (and the law school) or to ignore your studies to the detriment of your GPA.

Invariably what will happen is that you will get a wonderfully exciting project assigned that will have a deadline right smack in the middle of finals. You might have committed to doing something that could dramatically improve someone's life (housing, money, justice, freedom), and you will be caught between keeping your commitments and studying for final exams. You do not want to have that conflict.

You probably will have to prioritize your client commitments, but it will have a cost that lasts throughout law school. Before you commit to extracurricular obligations, make sure you plan out the realistic time commitments ahead and make sure you can handle them.

Attend Law School Events

Law schools offer a vibrant intellectual community. Law schools host fascinating speakers, panels, symposia, and lots of professional development sessions. The recipe for intellectual excitement can be found in every law school events calendar:

> one group of super-smart students
> a dozen student-led groups
> a sprinkle of engaged law professors
> a space for intellectual discussion and debate
> *Stir and wait for ideas to rise*

Seeing the law school as an incredibly rich and rewarding educational opportunity outside of class will deepen the classwork you do. Yes, there are costs with regard to studying and preparing for exams, but these types of events help strengthen the school community. Participate when you can. Even just being present can open doors that you did not know existed.

You should take advantage of the opportunities that happen right inside the law school every week. You can also usually find free food.

RULE 70

To Be a World-Changing Lawyer, You Have to Become a Lawyer First

There exists a hard balance to strike between activism in law school, intellectual engagement, and studying. Don't forget school comes first.

When you arrive at law school, there will be plenty of opportunities to engage in activism. Most will even center on noble and worthy causes. The problems are undeniable and urgent, and the cost of not engaging seems almost cruel. As stated, there will also be amazingly interesting programs of scholars, speakers, and issues. Every day there will be a distraction—and a choice about whether to engage in activism or study. You should participate. You should engage. You should learn. But understand that the costs are real.

It is not an easy choice about what to prioritize. But remember, to be a world-changing lawyer, you have to be a lawyer first. At least as a 1L, you need to focus on being a student first. You will not develop the skills to change the world without the hard and, honestly, more boring work of studying. That is your task. These are your tools.

Culture/
Community

The Rule of Professional Reputation

All law school graduates remember what their fellow law students did "that time" in class. Decades might pass, but you will be that student who did that thing.

Being a lawyer is all about maintaining and promoting a reputation for being a professional who is a problem-solver. This process doesn't start when you graduate and pass the bar examination. It starts the moment you sit down in your first law school class. Think about the image you want to project as a lawyer every time you open your mouth or interact with fellow students and professors. Any of them could be a future client or judge. They will take away a positive impression or a negative impression based on these interactions.

As such, learn to disagree without being disagreeable. Know that among reasonable minds, there will always be room for arguments different from your own. Understand that the value of your reputation is greater than the value of winning any single argument.

Maintain your principles and your honor. Advocate for your beliefs. But be civil. Be empathetic. Be fair. Be kind. You cannot undo the impression that your classmates or professors will have of you once you've lashed out or behaved in an inappropriate manner.

Expectations of Excellence

You have one chance to learn the law. Why would you shortchange yourself and your future clients? Every time you skip a class or a case or do less than the best you can do, you undermine your own expectations of excellence.

Help build a culture of excellence. Make it unacceptable to be unprepared for class or late. Make it a practice to join the debate and speak. Make it a habit to engage the material at a level of precision, depth, and nuance so that you feel like you own it. Set aside enough time to do the assignments in a way that will make you feel proud. Last-minute efforts or halfhearted attempts are not excellent and are not the stuff of excellent lawyers. They are not who you want to be as a lawyer.

Any lawyer in any law school can be the best lawyer in their city if they work hard enough. You must establish your own internal standards of excellence and work to achieve them. You are building a "brand" as a lawyer, and it starts in law school. You may not be able to change your peers in law school. You may not be able to change your law school. But you can change your own expectations and raise them high enough to excel.

Civic Health

Systems of law require institutions to support them. In a democracy, civic institutions must be cultivated to uphold shared values. Law school requires a similar commitment to civic health.

You can help build supportive institutions in your law school. You can create informal support networks. Study groups, study sessions, and support across the classes can be helpful in developing a culture of mutual success. Even just being kind to others throughout the day can help.

A strong law school community infused with civic values is built on mutuality, reciprocity, respect, engagement, and uplift. This is not just with your classmates but with the law school administration, staff, and everyone who works in the institution.

It also requires work. Self-government, civic connection, and community are all based on someone doing the hard work. You have to do the hard work (in addition to everything else). It is really easy as a 1L to retreat to a self-centered, school-focused you, but there is an institution around you that also needs attention.

The civic health of your law school depends on you. Your attitude in class, the respect you show to other classmates, the gratitude you give those who work for you in the school—that is the measure of a healthy institution.

Build Bridges to the Community

Law schools exist within a larger community. Yet, as a result of the pressures that come from studying, working, and learning the law, it is incredibly easy to ignore the surrounding world. Don't. Don't close off the community.

In law school, make two commitments to your community. Promise yourself you will attend at least one law-related community-based event a year and join one event that brings people from the community into the law school. You can do more, of course, but try to maintain some connection to the community that supports the law school.

Find ways through community service or volunteer opportunities or just human conversation to engage those who live right outside the law school. A law school education can narrow your vision to books, rules, and exams. But it can also expand your vision to how the law impacts the lives in the surrounding community. Building bridges to that community will enrich your legal education (and provide a bit of perspective).

RULE 75

Represent the Legal Profession and
Your Law School

You are now in a professional school. When you enter a law school or enter the legal profession, people expect a level of professionalism. How you present yourself and how you conduct yourself are now reflections of your law school and the legal profession.

- If you go to court, see yourself as a representative of the law school.
- If you meet a lawyer or a judge at an event, see yourself as a representative of the law school.
- If you participate in a moot court or other competition, see yourself as a representative of the law school.
- If you interview for a job, see yourself as a representative of the law school.
- If you meet a client, see yourself as a representative of the law school.

You are more than a student. You are part of an institution. You represent that institution.

Self-Care

Remove the Drama

Take care of business, family, and other drama before you start 1L year. 1L year is not the time to sort through long-simmering relationship conflicts or handle family business or really do anything else. No vacations in the middle of the semester. No family reunions. No unnecessary distractions.

Simplify your life. You have two goals: (1) be happy; (2) study and work to the best of your capabilities. That's it.

In order to remove the drama, you need to explain to family and non-law-school friends your priorities for 1L year. You are not insulting them. You are not minimizing their needs. You are just focused on something else. You must have this talk. They will not understand why the work is different. They will see it as "school," and you have done "school" before. But law school is different in scale, scope, time, and pressure. Your family must understand this at the beginning. No exceptions, no excuses (until holiday break). Explain it. Stand by it. You will be much happier (see goal 1).

RULE 77

Find Perspective

Law school is all-consuming. Classes, exams, a new career, and a thousand different things pulling at you can make it feel like you are losing control. Before you lose it, take a step back.

First, you are in law school—its own accomplishment.

Second, you will have a long legal career. An awkward answer in class or a bad grade in 1L year is not disqualifying from anything. Many amazing and successful lawyers messed up a class or two.

Third, the work is manageable. Yes, it is a lot. Yes, the demands do not let up. Yes, it takes effort to manage the flow. But every year approximately forty thousand students do exactly what you are doing and survive. You can do it too.

Fourth, the traditional success metrics in law school (grades, law review membership, awards) do not define you and do not mean that much over your career. They are like decorations on a birthday cake, nice but not the reason you want the cake. Work hard but keep perspective. Also, eat some cake.

Find Balance Every Day

You entered law school an accomplished person with a (somewhat) balanced life. The pressures and priorities of studying and other law school demands will erode that balance if you let them. Don't.

Find and maintain your balance. Find a moment of balance every day. Once a day, do something for yourself that has nothing to do with law school. Exercise, meditate, walk, sing, eat a cookie, call a friend, laugh, watch a TV show. Every day, find one thing that symbolizes balance in your life. Don't forget to prioritize these moments of balance every day.

Importantly, look for balance with the people you love (especially spouses, significant others, children). Law school kills relationships; it creates resentment, jealousy, and frustration. If you came into law school connected to someone you love, make a special effort to keep that bond strong. Law school will try to sever it. Finding time away from law school to reconnect and heal that bond is important if you want to keep it. If you are not intentional about strengthening this bond, the other pressures and demands that arise from the 1L experience will take over.

Avoid the Temptations

The statistics about lawyers and substance abuse are depressing. More than most professions, lawyers abuse drugs and alcohol. This substance abuse starts in law school. This substance abuse does not end in law school.

Part of self-care is seeing the temptations and justifying to yourself why they are not in your interest. There are drugs to focus, drugs to relax, drugs to escape. There are reasons to drown your sorrows. But remember that the lessons you learn to cope with law school stress will follow you as you cope with professional stress as a lawyer. You need to build constructive ways to handle it now, as a foundation for the future. The intensity of the 1L experience will wane, but other pressures will fill its place: the bar exam, your first job, your next job, the realities of clients, work, life. You must begin to establish your ability to succeed without the temptations of drugs or alcohol.

The legal profession has lost too many good people to addiction.

Help Is Here

Mental health crises happen in law school. Every law school has professionals who can help you in a crisis. Depression, suicidal thoughts, and emotional crises are common. You are not alone.

Mental health issues are routine for law school, and you can get help. Law school pressure exacerbates anxiety, panic attacks, and depression. Contact the dean of students or an appropriate administrator. Their job literally is to help you. They walk into work every morning waiting to help someone like you. It is not "a bother"; it is their job.

External crises will also happen in law school. Financial issues, criminal allegations, personal tragedies, and health problems are all relatively routine events in the life of a law school. You would not be the first person to run out of money or be arrested. You would not be the first person to lose a loved one or face a health issue. Again, contact the dean of students or an appropriate administrator. Their job is to help you.

You do not have to struggle through a crisis alone. Law school counselors can make what seems like an impossible situation manageable and maybe even okay. And if you could spy behind the closed office door of any dean of students, you would know you are not alone.

Midterms

Understand the Purpose of a Midterm

Not all classes have midterms, but for those that do, it is important to understand the purpose of a midterm. Midterms are assessments, midpoint check-ins to see if you are beginning to grasp the substance of a law school subject, as well as the process of how to take an exam. Consider it a practice exam to see if you can apply the law you are learning. Remember: application, application, application.

While midterms matter because they probably impact your final grade, they really matter more as an assessment of how you are doing in the course. Think of a midterm as a self-check to see if you really understand what you think you understand, and treat studying for it as a self-check on your study habits.

Think of it also as a practice run for how to attack a final law school exam. If you have never decoded a hypothetical issue-spotting question before the final, you will fail—not because you don't know the law but because you don't know how to take an exam. Midterms provide the practice.

RULE 82

Carve Out Time to Study

Midterm exams show up in the middle of your class schedule. You are given comparatively little time to study. Readings for other classes continue. Assignments for other courses keep coming. Unlike finals, for which you might have a full reading period to study, midterms happen right in the middle of ordinary life.

Despite the reality, you must find time to study. This does not just mean reread your notes. This does not just mean reread your outline. It means you must take practice tests. It means you need to shift your mind to applying the law. The more you practice taking law school exams, the better you will get—not simply because through practice you will understand the law better but because through practice you will see how the exams are designed.

Find past exams of your professor (most law school libraries make them available). Find other exams on the same subject (it doesn't matter from where). Most importantly, study the sample answers for structure.

Too many students take midterms blind to the reality of a law school exam's structure and purpose. They know the cases but not the rules. They know the issues but not how to apply IRAC to the problem. They know the law, but not how to apply the law. Only by studying and practicing law school exams will you master the game.

Trick Your Memory

Exams require you to memorize legal rules with different elements. There are lots of rules, and you need to be able to recall the elements quickly and correctly. Finding shortcuts to be able to easily categorize and organize the massive amount of information is key.

One trick is to use the RULE (remember, understand, law, easily) method to create acronyms and mnemonic phrases for each legal rule. These acronyms and mnemonic phrases create a checklist so you remember each component part. Associate the factor with a letter of the phrase. The more outlandish and shocking the acronym or mnemonic phrase, the more it will trigger your memory of the rule. This tip is applicable to all legal concepts and doctrines as well.

Another trick is to create flash cards to test yourself on elements. Although they may seem old-fashioned (like the stuff you might do in high school), if the test is based in part on memorizing, flash cards are great.

A final trick is to go to bed with the subject. One of the ways our brains work is to internalize things as we sleep. If you study a subject or memorize a rule definition right before you go to sleep, studies show that you can retain that information the next day and beyond.

You will find what works best for you. But find tricks to get the material in your head so you can spit it back on a piece of paper on the midterm.

Understand Issue-Spotting Exams

Not all midterm exams are issue-spotting exams. Some professors use multiple choice, essay, or a problem approach. But issue-spotting exams cause problems for 1Ls because they are unlike other types of exams you might have had in college.

Issue-spotting exams involve a hypothetical fact pattern in which students are expected to find the legal issues and analyze the applicable law. When you first come across such an exam, you might be paralyzed with trying to figure out where to start. So here is a guide.

The overall goal is to spot the legal issue, demonstrate you know the legal rule that governs the issue, analyze the rule on the basis of the facts given, and conclude with an answer. This is the IRAC method. Here is a handy way to think about the task at hand:

I: In every fact pattern there will be legal issues.

R: Every legal issue spotted has a rule. Every rule can be broken into elements.

A: Every element needs an argument from the facts.

C: Your argument needs a conclusion.

Just repeat this process over and over as you work through the facts.

RULE 85

Review Your Midterm

The single biggest mistake students can make with a midterm is not to review it after they take it. Whether you aced it or bombed it, the review part of the midterm is the key to doing well on the final.

Reread the problem, reread the question, reread your answer, and read any sample answer prepared. Understanding your mistakes, assumptions, conclusions, and errors is probably the best way to improve on the final.

Here is why. The midterm is just a shorter version of the final exam. Pay attention to what you do well or poorly. If timing is your problem on the midterm, timing will be your problem on the final. If analysis is your problem on the midterm, analysis will be your problem on the final. The tests are similar, and so are your problems with the test.

Too few students approach the midterm as a teaching moment, and too few learn from it. Good or bad, confidence building or demoralizing, the results of your midterm can help you improve on the final. And most people improve.

Equally importantly, you should speak with your professor after your midterm. Whether you did well or poorly (but especially if you did poorly), you should go seek guidance. Too many students do not go to their professors when they are struggling, perhaps embarrassed about the situation. Those are the students who should seek out help. Your confusion can be fixed. You will not be judged. Seek help with your professors and the academic success professionals in your school.

Reading Period

Focus on the Future, Not the Past

Having just spent a semester learning several difficult subjects, you now have a week (or so) to get ready for all of your exams. Your first inclination might be to reread all your class materials, but in truth you cannot. There is too much information to go back and reread cases or review all of your notes.

Instead, you must prepare for the future exam. You must take the foundational issues, rules, elements, and analyses and operationalize them for the future exam. Your studying should be forward looking and targeted to the information that will show up on the exam. It obviously will be based on past knowledge and review, but the focus should be on application.

Reading period signifies the end of classes. Use it as a moment to change your orientation from the past to the future. All that matters is figuring out how to attack the exam. Concentrate on identifying the issues, mastering the elements of the rules, and seeing how the issues flow together in any subject.

Practice Taking Practice Exams

The best way to practice taking an exam is to take an exam. Practice exams are critical to turning background knowledge into exam answers. Just as you did with midterms, you must do so again with finals.

You must leave time to take, study, deconstruct, and review as many practice exams as you can. Let's put it even more bluntly: if you do not practice actually taking final exams, you will do poorly.

Everyone can remember the first time they sat down and looked at their first law school hypothetical exam question. It involves a feeling of paralysis, confusion, and wonder. You do not want this feeling in the actual exam. You want to study how exams are constructed. You want to study how answers are organized. You want to have gone through the humbling failure of answering an exam question well before the actual final exam. You want to master the game of taking law school exams before exam period.

And it is a game. Figure out the game of what the professor is asking for and win. Exams are not about intelligence. They are not about naturally talented lawyers. They are a game that you can master. By studying old exams (from any professor), you will begin seeing how the subject flows, where the issues lie, and how to apply the law you know to the facts you have just read.

Strategize Flow

By the time reading period arrives, you should have an outline of the important issues, the rules that accompany those issues, and a general framework on how those issues fit together. During reading period, you want to focus on the way the issues fit together. In a criminal law class, see crimes, defenses, excuses, and so on. In a civil procedure class, see how a case develops through the rules.

You need to begin organizing your thinking so you can strategize through the problem presented. You will not know the exam question, but you should be able to know the formula to attack any question.

Think of each course as a flow chart of issues. A factual scenario will be presented, and you need to apply this issue-spotting process to the facts. Any exam question can be fit into the flow, because the issues you have learned do not change. Those issues will fit, and the question is only how.

RULE 89

Create Issue Checklists

Think about what a final exam is to the professor. It represents an opportunity to see if you learned the material taught in the class. This is a test to show what you know. In a 1L class, there exists a finite amount of information to test. The issues are cabined to those you studied, the rules limited to those you covered. In many cases, there is even a formula to the analysis. That is what you need to focus on for exam prep.

Before any exam, you should make a list of possible issues. Create a checklist to make sure you do not miss any. Then when you are taking the exam, scan it for possible issues. Remember that issues may have subissues and may give rise to defenses, but study the exam looking for places to put the issues you know.

You should be able to make a mental checklist of issues as you read through a fact pattern. In a final exam, check off these issues so that in the heat of the moment, you don't miss any important arguments.

RULE 90

Pre-write Answers

Along with your issue checklist, you should memorize the rules that go along with any issue, such that you know if you see that issue, you will write down the following rule. You can almost pre-write answers for most exams, because you know that certain issues almost have to appear, and if they do, those rules will appear.

If the game of exam taking is spotting the issues (using the checklist), filling in the rule, and then applying the facts provided in the question to the rule, then two out of the three steps (issue, rule) can be done ahead of time. Think about that: you can pre-write two-thirds of your final exam if you think about what you will write for each issue.

Of course, the analysis matters, the defenses or counter-arguments matter, and the ability to use relevant facts matters. Professors are not going to make it too easy on you. But you can get ahead of the game by thinking through the nuggets of knowledge you will drop when you see each issue.

.

Final Exams

A Word about Stress

Exams equal stress. You can feel it in the air of a law school, when for several weeks the final-exam-generated tension is palpable and unavoidable.

There is a reason for the stress. You are being asked to synthesize too much information about too many subjects in too little time. Even if you have followed all the rules in this book, you will be stressed. No one can tell you to avoid stress or use stress to focus in a way that will be helpful. Stress is not helpful or avoidable.

But you can plan for it, put it in context, and not let it take over your life. You will walk into each final exam stressed. You will also walk out of that exam. And no matter how you do on the actual exam, you will be fine. Millions of lawyers have done it, and you will too.

Taking care of yourself as you approach exams is critically important. It seems cruel to suggest getting enough sleep, eating right, and exercising at a time when everyone knows those luxuries of life are nearly impossible with the amount of work expected. But sleeping helps your thinking. Exercise clears the mind. Eating is necessary for your body. If you plan ahead, you can find ways to destress and take care of yourself. And if you didn't plan ahead, don't worry; you will survive.

The Call of the Question

Read the questions before you read the facts. When you first read the exam, skip to the actual questions at the end. How many questions are there? How much time per question? Read the call of the question carefully. Take a moment to think. Strategize an answer. Don't jump right into the facts before you have thought through your strategy based on the questions. Don't skip over a question. (It happens. It shouldn't.) Five minutes of strategizing is worth twenty minutes of panicked writing.

Words matter. Your professors have spent time crafting the questions to test your knowledge. They have added time suggestions to indicate what type of answer they expect. They have written the questions to keep you from complaining that they were unfair after the fact. They have written the questions carefully to get you to see certain issues and make certain arguments. Exam drafting is a skill, and the words chosen matter. Read carefully and think about why the words were used. The call of the question can be a helpful clue.

Think "Where," Not "What"

Law school exams are not real. You are not solving a real-world legal issue. You are being tested on whether you mastered the assigned material.

When you see an exam question asking you to analyze a factual scenario, realize that this is merely the setup to demonstrate your knowledge of the law. There are only so many issues discussed in any class, and the professor is going to test you on some/most of them.

Your professor taught you the rules of the subject, so odds are you are going to be tested on those rules. You need to look for where in the facts they appear. Go through the facts and circle all the issues—all the places you can put your knowledge of the rules to work. Don't worry about actually solving the legal issue. Your goal is to show that you understand the legal issues around the subject, as evinced by your IRAC for each issue buried in the fact pattern.

Packaging an Exam Answer

To succeed in class, you need to know the facts, the issues, the rules, and the outcome for every case. As we discussed, the rule is buried like a well-wrapped present inside the cases you read.

To succeed on the final exam, you don't need the wrapping, just the gift inside. You need to invert the focus of your reading to pull out the rule that you will apply when you see the issue in the facts. Too many students think in terms of cases rather than rules. Cases are nice to cite to show that you understand where the rule came from, but for exams, rules matter.

After the rule, you need to analyze the facts. Do not forget the analysis part. Too many students assume the analysis without showing their work. You don't get credit for the right answer unless your analysis shows why you got to that right answer. As stated, some of this can be done before you see the exam. Think of it as prepackaged IRAC answers for the legal issues you know you are going to be tested on.

Time for an A

Timing matters. Most law students could ace final exams with unlimited time. Most 1L exams are timed exams. The bar exam is a timed exam. Working within time constraints is challenging, perhaps unfair, and definitely harder. But it is a skill to learn like all the other skills of law school.

Every year, students make the same mistake of spending too much time on the first few questions and failing to leave time for the last questions. They answer that first question wonderfully well but then run out of time to finish the exam. Timing matters, and you don't get a good grade if you don't answer all the questions. Every year good students do poorly because they fail to account for time.

Time yourself on practice exams. Stick to a firm time allotment in the exam. You do not get points for blank pages, so you must complete the exam. The excuse that "I am slow" or "I am a bad typist," while perhaps true, is unhelpful. It is also one of the easiest things to work to improve. High-school-aged children now type faster than anyone ever. If you didn't learn it in high school, you still can. And you probably should, because law school exams are partially a comparison against what other students write. Being slow can be a competitive disadvantage.

Second Semester
and Beyond

RULE 96

Review the Semester

Once you survive the fall semester of 1L year, you never want to look back. This feeling is completely understandable and completely counterproductive. You just learned a ton. You learned a new language, a new way of thinking, new substantive rules, and new professional expectations all in a few short months. Now is the time to reflect on how you did it and how you can do it better.

- Did your outlines work for you?
- Did you save enough time to take practice exams and study?
- Did you lose time on something not productive?
- Did you manage the stress?

Take an hour of your winter break and reflect. Talk to others about what worked for them. Make another Day One plan for next semester. You will not make the same mistakes the second semester if you take a time-out to reflect now.

RULE 97

Professional Advancement

Learning the law of law school is not just about grades and exams. It also involves learning about the hidden markers of prestige and access in the legal profession.

- Spend time thinking about whether you would want a clerkship working with a judge upon graduation.
- Spend time in the career services offices finding out about the various fellowships, job placement options, and paths in law.
- Spend time figuring out how to prioritize the opportunities available to you at the law school. Many of the opportunities start much earlier than you would think.

Develop mentors from the faculty and administration and in the larger legal community who can explain and identify the markers for you. Your plan will change, but start thinking about a possible path the next year and beyond.

In a few short years, you will need these people to open doors, flag your accomplishments, and get you off the pile of applications for the next step of your career.

Law Review and Other Leadership Positions

As you peek over the horizon to your 2L and 3L years, take a look at what other students are doing. Why would a student join the law review or be an editor of a scholarly journal? Law reviews are student-run journals that publish scholarly articles that law students edit. Traditionally, membership on the law review (or other journals) has been associated with top academic and writing skills. As a result, being an editor on a law review (or a law journal) is seen as a marker of success in law school. What are the clinical offerings available? Clinical programs allow students to work with real clients on real cases. Clinical programs allow supervised lawyering before graduation. What leadership positions exist that might help differentiate you from the larger law student pack? State and local bar associations offer leadership positions to law students. Your law school needs students to run student programs and participate in faculty committees. Think about joining them.

Fortunately, you do not have to do anything but begin asking questions at this moment before 1L spring semester, but you also do not want to let a future opportunity pass you by. The pressure ramps up again in the spring, and you will bury your head again. Start asking about why your fellow students have chosen a path and what you can do to follow in it. Make sure you know of any deadlines in the spring so you can be sure to meet them.

Congratulate Yourself

You survived 1L fall semester. You did it. You will survive the spring semester and the next year and the next. Take a moment to congratulate yourself. You did it.

Repeat

Okay, congratulation time is over. Time to repeat the one hundred rules again—and again for each semester. Review. Repeat. It gets easier each time.

Conclusion

This book is just a starting point—a way of framing the rules for law school success. Like a constitution, parts are meant to be read literally, and other parts offer first principles for your own interpretation.

As law students, you are the interpreters of your own experience, and you will create your own common law understanding. Every year, there is a new generation of students coming behind you, and every year these rules need to be retaught, reexamined, and remade into a black-letter understanding of success.

This understanding will also change over time and evolve, school to school, year to year. There is no code to succeed, just the accumulated wisdom of many similarly situated students over time. Please add to this list, share it, and build up other students around you. The law of law school is not a secret and should be widely shared by all who can benefit.

JONATHAN YUSEF NEWTON'S STORY

I wish I had had this book before my first day of law school. This information would have helped eliminate much of the self-doubt, anxiety, and heartache of that first year. For the most part, law school and the law are an insider's game. What you don't know about law school necessarily causes you to lose and lose big. Like many of my classmates, I was an outsider trying to learn the inside game of law school.

I showed up enthusiastic and excited but ill prepared and anxious. To add to that, even in my forties, I had a ton of self-doubt and self-defeating habits. I had the desire and the discipline, but I lacked the knowledge of the game. By the time our first midterm exam grades came out, my enthusiasm and excitement turned into fear. In some of my classmates, it was outright panic. We didn't know what was really going on or what to do about it. The "teaching" of law was obscure and "different." Questions in class were answered with more questions. The fast-paced Socratic method led some students to withdraw and hide for fear of embarrassment. I wouldn't wish that anguish and experience on anyone.

Instead of becoming a victim in what some of my classmates called "Socratic torture," I started observing and taking note of what was really happening. When they taught us to question everything, I took it literally and started questioning the entire process of law school. What were they really teaching us? What was the benefit of this method? What could I do as a student to make my learning experience more effective and impactful for myself? Many of the answers came shortly after final exams of my first year (in other words, too late). As I and some of my classmates wrestled with the process, I developed some rules and phrases to help myself and other students during my next year. In my 2L year, I partnered with some of my schoolmates to develop a student-led learning collaboration to share our experiences and methods. By the end of my third year, I was tutoring a handful of first-year law students. I thought everyone should know the material and information I had. Eventually, my efforts caught the attention of Professor Ferguson, and we developed the idea of this guide to the 1L experience.

This book is, we hope, a mixture of inspirational and informational material. As you will soon learn, knowing and mastering the black-letter law is only part of the game. It is a necessary part of the game but not sufficient to real success. To be honest, knowing the law is actually the easier part of the entire process. As we have shared with you, what we have come to call "the law of law school" is the harder part. First, you must understand the process, expectations, and tricks to law school success. Second, you must understand that to dominate this game, you must know and master yourself. The first obstacle in your path to becoming a successful law student is yourself: your habits, your discipline, your willingness to self-motivate and to reflect on your strengths and weaknesses and to make adjustments. I was unprepared for several reasons. I came to law school carrying the mental baggage of self-doubt and messages of defeat. If that self-doubt and self-defeat is part of your background, you must first dispel the notion that you cannot be a successful law student right now. Understanding my journey and background may help you with yours.

In the admissions game of law school, the broad classification given to law students like me is "nontraditional." We can define that classification by observing more traditional law school students. Simply put, traditional law applicants are middle- to upper-class students in their midtwenties who matriculated more or less straight from undergrad to law school. Using these criteria, I could be classified as a nontraditional outsider's outsider. My path to law school was an improbable and unlikely journey.

In August 2013, at the age of forty-one, I had just completed my undergraduate degree in social science. I started and finished a bachelor's degree in just sixteen months. Later in that same month, a thirteen-count felony indictment against me was dismissed by prosecutors. I had been criminally charged in 2011 and had been out on bond for twenty-six months. The full story is for another book. But the short version is that before law school, I was a police officer. I blew the whistle on a sitting sheriff, and the blowback was a litany of false criminal charges. While I was out on bail, my lawyer half jokingly suggested I should consider going to law school. I quite seriously replied, "If I don't go to prison, I'll go to law school." And I did.

I went straight from undergrad to law school and was decidedly nontraditional—a middle-aged African American male with a family and an upbringing that was anything but upper-middle class. I am the son of a twice-convicted felon. My mother was a late bloomer who went to nursing school at age thirty-five. While my father was incarcerated, my brother and I grew up in my grandmother's house, with an alcoholic grandfather and a certified schizophrenic uncle. The six of us shared a 1,056-square-foot home in Key West, Florida. My living conditions contributed to making my elementary and high school academic record less than stellar. After my father's first incarceration, we moved from Key West to Hinesville, Georgia, back to Key West and then finally to Augusta, Georgia. I attended two middle schools and three high schools. I was held back in the seventh and tenth grades. I graduated high school at age twenty. If there was a class vote for the person least likely to be lawyer, I would have captured every vote.

I put all of my background out there up front to empower you, to encourage and inform you that law school and becoming a lawyer is not only possible but probable if you learn the law of law school. Most people with a background like mine would have given up on their dream and moved on to something else. But for those who are resilient, who have grit and determination, and to all the outsiders like me, this book was written for you. I am currently a proud law school graduate and member of the Maryland Bar.

ANDREW GUTHRIE FERGUSON'S STORY

This book began with tears. Every year, 1L students come to my office in tears. The tears are not because they failed a class or an exam (although they may have) but because they failed themselves. Through the tears, they realize that they approached 1L year all wrong and want another chance. I have seen the tears so many times that I can almost predict the reasons for the failure—a disappointment that has nothing to do with intelligence, grit, or legal aptitude. It almost always has to do with planning, organization, and understanding the expectations of the first one hundred days in law school. This book arose quite selfishly to avoid more of those conversations. If you understand the rules to succeed in law school, you actually will succeed in law school and beyond.

I am admittedly not the perfect person to write a book about struggling in law school. I went to an elite law school, had two lawyers as parents, and have had all the insider knowledge one might imagine during law school. I bought two or three study guides for each class, outlined hard, took as many practice exams as I could, and pretty much did what was expected of me to do well in law school. What I never asked myself, however, was why I knew what to do to succeed. When did I get "the memo"? The truth is that I didn't get an actual memo, but somehow through my privilege and life experience, I knew what to do to succeed.

When I started as a law professor, it struck me that so many students didn't have this insider's insight. Many students were unaware of how law schools test knowledge or the resources available to them in addition to the classroom and the casebook. In fact, many students did not recognize that law school is designed in a completely different way from other educational experiences. And the true tragedy of the situation is that eventually after the tears, after the self-doubt, these same students realized how they could have done better. These students had more creativity, resilience, and mental toughness than anyone I knew but just needed to channel those strengths to the appropriate task.

I started listening to these students, jotting down notes about missed opportunities, confusion about expectations, and just the disorienting way law is taught. Over my decade of teaching law, I kept a running list of rules, trying to suggest to my students how to think about what law school is actually teaching and testing (and how law professors "hide the ball" on many of these things).

I realized that the same frustrations I witnessed had been happening for decades. Students would show up to law school. They would diligently go to class, read cases, figure out arcane facts, and then after an entire semester of case-based class discussion be given one final exam that did not focus on cases or the Socratic questions discussed in class. Instead, they were asked to analyze a series of hypothetical fact patterns that only indirectly involved the cases or the debates in class. Students who followed the rules of the game left baffled that there were other rules to follow for the exam. Sadly, these students only figured out the game of law school in subsequent semesters. This was the frustrating experience of many smart, talented law students who just had not been given a clue about what to expect on 1L exams. They did not know that merely following the in-class game wouldn't be enough to succeed because there were hidden rules and advantages to be found.

I decided I wanted to figure out a way to make anyone who comes to law school an "insider." I wanted to reveal the "game" of law school (or at least 1L year) so that everyone can compete on an equal playing field.

One day, a 3L student stopped by my office and started talking about how he was frustrated that he had not done as well as he could his first year in law school. He started articulating the same frustrations of many of the law students who didn't get the memo. He was a nontraditional student, older, and without lawyers in his family, and no one told him what to expect. But he had answers. He had solutions and slogans and plans to change things. In fact, as a 3L student leader, he had been organizing a group of 1L students himself to help them avoid the pitfalls that befell him. He was passionate, real, and smart. He understood what it took to turn insight into practice.

Jonathan Yusef Newton and I decided to write this book at that moment. Collectively, we knew we could speak across barriers of race, class, education, and experience and to a wide world of law students about the fundamental rules that lead to law school success. This book is our shared vision of those core rules.

ABOUT THE AUTHORS

ANDREW GUTHRIE FERGUSON is a law professor and the author of *The Rise of Big Data Policing* and *Why Jury Duty Matters*.

JONATHAN YUSEF NEWTON is an attorney at the Law Office of Jonathan Y. Newton, LLC.